STRANGE STUFF

True Stories
of Odd Places and Things

By

JANET NUZUM MYERS

Illustrations by
Maj-Britt Hagsted

1999
LINNET BOOKS

First published 1999 as a Linnet Book,
an imprint of The Shoe String Press, Inc.,
2 Linsley Street, North Haven, Connecticut 06473.

Library of Congress Cataloging-in-Publication Data

Myers, Janet Nuzum, 1940–
   Strange stuff : true stories of odd places and things /
by Janet Nuzum Myers ; illustrations by Maj-Britt Hagsted.
      p.   cm.
   Includes index.
   Summary: Kids love to contemplate strange stuff. Quicksand is
right up there with Bigfoot, the Bermuda Triangle, meat–eating
plants, the lost continent of Atlantis, wolf children, voodoo and
zombies, scorpions and tarantulas, black holes, and more. The
myths and the truth as we know them are here in this grab bag
collection of weird stuff designed to pique the insatiable curiosity
of children. And to get them thinking.
   ISBN 0-208-02405-0 (cloth/ library : alk. paper)
   1. Science—Miscellanea—Juvenile literature.
I. Hagsted, Maj-Britt. II. Title.
Q173.M9826   1999   98-52389
001.94—DC21   CIP

The paper in this publication meets the minimum requirements of
American National Standard for Information Science—Permanence of
Paper for Printed Library Materials, ANSI Z39.48–1984. ♾

Designed by Sanna Stanley

Printed in the United States of America

*To
Warren,
Laura, Craig, Darin,
and Edyth*

Contents

Contents

Preface

In our fascinating world we find so many places and things that we describe with words like "awesome," "weird," or "far-out." Some subjects never fail to spark our interest. Other topics cause our imaginations to skyrocket. From aardvarks to zombies, the themes are countless. It's fun to soak up facts about captivating places and things.

This book is a sampling of strange stuff—odd places and things to wonder about. Some are mysterious; some will leave you wondering if they are "for real."

Enter the world of strange stuff:

- **Decide** if you should worry about zombies
- **Learn** why some mysteries like Bigfoot and the Bermuda Triangle are still unsolved
- **Explore** the creepy world of scorpions and tarantulas, and get to know some meat-eating plants
- **Discover** the whereabouts of treasure that refuses to be claimed, and investigate the possibility of mermaids
- **Journey** to black holes in space
- **See** how feral children have lived
- **Get acquainted** with snake charmers, up close and personal

- **Visit** a continent that may, or may not, have existed
- **Find out** how to get unstuck from quicksand

Things that happen in real life are often unbelievable. The chapters in this book are based on fact, but you must judge if enough evidence exists to believe the amazing stories.

You can find out more about any of these "strange stuff" topics from the bibliography of titles listed in the back of this book. Enjoy them, and others, in your local library.

1
How Dangerous Is Quicksand?

Opinions about quicksand are often formed by its shadowy reputation. Remember this scene? It's been in countless movies.

The camera zooms in on a man plodding through the jungle, alone. From the eerie music you know something bad is about to happen. Chills creep up your spine as the shrill music grows louder. With a shocked scream the man suddenly plunges up to his waist in a brown ooze. Quicksand! He struggles to get free. The more he thrashes his arms, the faster he sinks. He cries out again. Birds and monkeys stop their noisy chirping and chattering. They listen to his shrieks. The squishy mass slowly swallows the man, and then silence spreads through the jungle.

In movies and books, quicksand causes a terrible and certain death like this for anyone unlucky enough to stumble into it. But, is this really how it is?

To answer that, we must find out: What exactly is quicksand? It starts as ordinary fine sand. It becomes dangerous when the sand mixes with water gushing upward through the sand. Underground springs are often the culprits, causing the sand to swell and lose its firmness. It can't support heavy weight.

Quicksand is most commonly found near streams and riverbanks. A sandbar along a stream may look firm, but if it has water rushing up through it, look out! Sometimes a dry riverbed is covered with a thin crust that camouflages unstable sand.

What really happens when people tangle with quicksand? An environmental scientist had this experience while on a California field trip. He was walking along a creek, and then stepped onto what appeared to be a sandbar. Suddenly the man sank up to his waist in a sludge of sandy water. He tore off his small backpack and tossed it onto the bank. Within seconds he swam to firm ground and lunged out of the mire. The scientist found that the pockets and seams of his clothes were crammed with sand. He would have been pulled down by the added weight if he hadn't reacted so swiftly.

The scientist's speedy and successful exit was unusual. This is what is more likely to happen if you step into quicksand. You drop into what feels like a soupy, bottomless pit, then bob up to a level around your waist. The water causes you to float in the first few seconds. Then the sand fills your shoes and clothing. You start to sink. What do you do now?

Don't panic. Frantic struggles only make you sink faster. Fall backward with your arms and legs out-

stretched. This spreads your weight. In most cases, people can float on top of quicksand. Get rid of your shoes and equipment, such as backpacks. Have someone hand you a branch or a rope, and then slowly pull you out.

Even if you are alone, you can free yourself. Quicksand behaves like an extremely thick liquid. Moving in it is like swimming slow motion—in pudding. Slowly, very slowly, you can slither to solid ground.

If the gooey sandpit creates a strong suction, you can expect your escape to take a long time. In Colorado, one survivor inched a distance of ten feet in eight hours to squirm out of a pool of quicksand.

It has a nasty reputation, but quicksand is not responsible for many human deaths. Large animals like cows are more common victims. They panic, sink fast, and drown. Some people have lost their lives in quicksand, but its perils have been greatly exaggerated in books and movies.

Although quicksand is found in all fifty states, it is likely that you will never come across it. But if you should ever find yourself in a quicksand-mess, stay calm. As with many of nature's dangers, your best defense is to understand what quicksand is and know how to deal with it. Wise actions come from knowledge.

2
Is Bigfoot
a Big Joke?

Descriptions of Bigfoot are consistent. It is:

- **huge** (7 to 9 feet tall and weighs 400–900 pounds)
- **furry** (usually dark brown shaggy hair)
- **apelike** (but curiously human)
- **an upright, walking creature** (with strides 6 to 8 feet long)
- **bad-smelling** (it stinks)
- **shy** (but can scream with an eerie shrill sound)
- **nocturnal** (but also active in daytime)

How can we prove that this being exists when we do not have a specimen, dead or alive? We have no skeletons—not even one bone. We have no photos—except for a few blurry images. Some of the photos are obvious fakes. For several years, Project Bigfoot in Seattle, Washington has offered a reward of $10,000 for proof, beyond a doubt, that Bigfoot exists. The reward remains uncollected.

In recent years the Bigfoot saga has been splattered with mockery. Bigfoot's likeness shows up in cartoons

and funny movies. The large furry critter is portrayed as dumb and powerful, but nonviolent. It's always open season for poking fun at Bigfoot. There's even a Bigfoot PIZZA for goodness sakes!

So, that's it. End of story. Bigfoot cannot be taken seriously. Bigfoot IS a big joke. Right?

Not quite.

Many people still believe there's more to the legend of Bigfoot. Why do they hang on to these beliefs? Bigfoot stories have been around for hundreds of years. From Northern California to Canada's British Columbia, the legend spread. Native American tribes shared tales of a strong, hairy man-beast. The Salish tribe of British Columbia called him Sasquatch, which means "wild man of the woods."

A president of the United States, Teddy Roosevelt, was a noted outdoorsman. He wrote a book, in 1893, called *The Wilderness Hunter.* Roosevelt described a large strange animal that walked on two legs, with footprints like a human, in the Pacific Northwest. He could not say what it was, but he was certain it was not a bear. Roosevelt did not see the animal himself, but he apparently believed the witnesses he interviewed.

Scattered stories swirled around for years, but in 1958 the upright, hairy beast gained worldwide fame.

Early one morning, in a remote area of Northern California, a road crew found huge footprints of a two-legged creature that had picked up 300-pound drums of fuel and tossed them around. The foreman made a cast of a footprint, and the crew nicknamed the night prowler "Bigfoot."

What started as a small local newspaper story expanded into a news report read around the world. Bigfoot was famous.

Since then many believers have ventured into the thick forests of the Pacific Northwest, searching for the elusive Bigfoot.

A 1967 sighting still stirs debate. Roger Patterson and Bob Gimlin were horseback riding in an isolated region in Northern California. Patterson had written a book about Bigfoot. Armed with a 16mm movie camera, he hoped to encounter the animal. Several footprints had previously been spotted in the area.

Suddenly, the horses became jittery. Patterson's frightened horse reared at the sight of a Bigfoot crossing a clearing ahead of them. Patterson was thrown from the horse. He frantically grabbed the movie camera, stumbled toward the Bigfoot, and began filming. The creature glanced over its shoulder at Patterson as it walked with rapid strides into the heavy brush, out of sight. A nervous Roger Patterson and Bob Gimlin did not try to follow.

For many people, this glimpse of a Bigfoot was all the proof they needed. The resulting 952 frames of color film revealed a 7 foot tall beast weighing about 400 pounds. Its dark furry body was topped by a dome-shaped head and human-like face.

Bob Gimlin said, "It's appearance was one of a large humanoid creature walking like a human being . . . There is no way this could ever be falsified or any person could be in a fur suit because of the movement of the muscle underneath the hair."

The film has been analyzed, frame by frame, by various experts. Some simply scoff at it. Others take it seriously. Some analysts think the movements were not made by a human or any member of the ape family.

Hundreds of footprint casts have been made since the Patterson film was presented. Sizes range from 14 to 24 inches long. The most startling footprint casts were made by a U.S. Forest Service patrolman in 1982. The man claimed he saw an 8 foot tall Bigfoot hurrying down a logging road. The footprint casts showed remarkable details of the dermal ridges—like fingerprints of the feet. These would be hard to fake, claim believers.

Bigfoot hair strands that had been found were analyzed by a biologist in Berkeley, California, in 1992. The scientist reported that the hair was related to the human-chimpanzee-gorilla group of primates, yet was different from any of these. "An unknown species," was his conclusion.

Getting a Bigfoot to pose for cameras has been a challenge. In 1992, again in Northern California, Daryl Owen and Scott Herriott videotaped a creature looking at them through the bushes. It was about 40 feet away and described as a "beige gorilla-man." The sound accompanying the video recorded the young men's tense conversation during their close encounter. Later the video images were expanded by a commercial video company. Professional video editors concluded only that some sort of being was shown on the tape. Once more, Bigfoot just granted a fuzzy view.

There is no solid evidence to prove that Bigfoot lives. But plenty of footprints and over two thousand eyewitness sightings have kept Bigfoot watchers trudging through the woods.

Fantastic yarns have been told by some individuals. A man named Albert Ostman kept his story secret for more than thirty years. Then Ostman claimed that he had been captured, in 1924, by a Bigfoot family—a mother, father, and two Bigfoot children. On the third day of captivity, Ostman offered the Bigfoot father some snuff. After eating the entire box of snuff, the Bigfoot became violently ill. The captive escaped during the confusion.

Not all tales are this dramatic. In 1988, two schoolteachers and their husbands camped in a secluded spot in a Canadian park. They stayed up late, playing cards. When they finally prepared to go to bed, after 1:00 A.M., they heard what they thought was a bear. The frightened couples bolted to their cars. In the glare of headlights, they were shocked to see a dark, hairy, 8 foot tall monster. With arms swinging, it rapidly walked through the flood of lights. The terrorized campers alerted park rangers. Each witness reported the exact same description during individual interviews.

The Pacific Northwest is not the only place that claims to be a home to a mysterious ape-person. Bigfoot may have cousins.

Thousands of miles away, in Asia's Himalaya mountains, a beast called *Yeti* is said to reside. We know it as the Abominable Snowman (another bad-smelling brute). Other countries, such as China and Russia, have legends of a Bigfoot-like creature. In China, the name is *Hsing-Hsing*, and in Russia it is called *Almas*. These beasts are described as similar to Bigfoot: upright walkers; covered with hair; dome-shaped heads; human-like. If they exist, how could these creatures be related?

A land bridge connected the continents of North America and Asia, over one hundred thousand years ago, where the Bering Strait is today. Ancestors of Native Americans crossed this land bridge to Alaska. They probably followed and hunted herds of animals. Bigfoot's ancestors could have spread from Asia to North America this way as well.

So what are we to believe? Is there enough evidence to support Bigfoot's existence? Doubters argue that it is unlikely that the creature could stay hidden from civilization. However, believers point out that this could happen in the heavily wooded areas of the Pacific Northwest. Small airplanes have crashed in these remote places. Sometimes the wreckage is never found in the thick tangle of trees and brush. In this expansive wilderness, a shy, solitary being could find plenty of cover.

What about skeletons? Why have no Bigfoot bones appeared? Maybe nature's scavengers answer that. In a dense woods it's unusual to find skeletons of dead animals. They are "recycled" by other animals. Various scavengers, from wolverines to beetles, eat everything from flesh to bones—keeping the forest floor tidy.

The bottom line, though, is that there is no concrete proof of Bigfoot's existence. Some skeptics call the creature a "UWO," an "Unidentified Walking Object." They assign Bigfoot to the category of strange stuff for people's dreams, or nightmares.

The debate goes on. Bigfoot seekers prowl the mountains and forests, on the lookout for clues. More footprints will be located and sightings will continue.

From time to time, around the globe, species of life new to us are discovered and presented to the human world. Whether we are believers or not, something inside us stirs at the possibility of Bigfoot being next on the list. Could it happen?

3
Does the Bermuda Triangle Deserve Its Bad Reputation?

Thousands of people journey through the Bermuda Triangle each day. Nothing unusual happens.

Why, then, do some people avoid going there? What causes them to regard the place as a backdrop for the Twilight Zone?

Lying off the coast of Florida in the Atlantic Ocean, the Bermuda Triangle is a big area, spreading over 440,000 square miles of ocean. Its imaginary points touch Florida, Puerto Rico, and the Bermuda Islands. On a map, it looks innocent enough—just a section of the ocean. So what goes on here?

Consider events of past years.

As early as Christopher Columbus's 1492 voyage from Europe to the New World, odd things occurred. While sailing in this region, Columbus and his crew watched a bright column of fire streak across the sky. The ship's compass started spinning wildly. The crew spotted glowing streaks of white on the ocean's surface. Columbus had to calm his panicky sailors.

Curiously, 500 hundred years later, orbiting American astronauts reported patches of light and foam on the ocean near this same location.

In this century, the Bermuda Triangle first exploded into the news in 1945. Around the world, newspaper headlines relayed details of a strange tragedy: an entire military air squadron had vanished. On a sunny afternoon, five U.S. Navy Avenger bombers carrying a total of fourteen crewmen left a Florida base for a routine training flight over the Atlantic Ocean. They were known as Flight 19, and their troubles began an hour into the mission.

The squadron leader, Lieutenant Charles Taylor, radioed, "We're lost . . . don't know which way is west. Everything is wrong . . . strange. We can't be sure of any direction . . . the ocean doesn't even look as it should!" After that, the air traffic controllers could only hear a few words of the pilots' messages through heavy radio static.

The ground crew listened helplessly for three hours while the confused Avenger bombers wandered off course. The aircraft instruments seemed to be giving crazy readings. After a final garbled message from Flight 19, there was silence.

Within an hour of Lieutenant Taylor's first frantic message, help was on the way. A large search plane flew from the base with a crew of thirteen. After reporting back to the base two times, this aircraft also disappeared.

Shocked military personnel launched a massive air/ sea rescue operation. Twenty ships and hundreds of

aircraft were unable to locate the six missing airplanes and crews totaling twenty-seven men.

After this unexplained disaster jolted the public, the Bermuda Triangle's past was examined. More sensational stories surfaced. For this area of the Atlantic, nicknamed the "Devil's Triangle" by some people, creepy tales came forth. Ships had been found that were abandoned at sea. Other ships seemed to be swallowed by the ocean in a big gulp—they simply disappeared.

In the mid-1800s, two large sailing ships hauling

cargo started the stir. A French ship, the *Rosalie*, was found drifting with full sails and no crew. A few years later an American ship, the *James B. Chester,* appeared in the same manner—everything in place, but the entire crew missing.

In 1880, a British training ship, the *Atalanta*, sailed from Bermuda and then completely vanished. Aboard were 290 people—mostly young boys who were learning to become sailors.

One of the spookiest stories about the Bermuda Triangle was told by the crew of another British ship, the *Ellen Austin*. Off the coast of Bermuda, the crew members of the *Ellen Austin* spied a drifting schooner (a sailing ship with two or more masts). When they boarded the schooner they found all items in place, including a valuable cargo. The only thing missing was the crew.

The captain of the *Ellen Austin* picked a new crew from his own men to sail the schooner to port. A violent storm separated the two ships. Two days later the schooner was sighted. The captain and sailors of the *Ellen Austin* learned, to their dismay, that once again there was no one on board. A new crew of volunteers now took over the phantom schooner. The two ships headed toward port. For a second time they became separated during a raging gale. When the skies cleared, the stunned sailors on the *Ellen Austin* stared wide-eyed in all directions at the open sea. The schooner was gone. No wreckage, no crew.

In 1918, a gigantic cargo steamship as long as two football fields met an unknown fate. The SS *Cyclops* was sailing from the West Indies to Virginia. A final message from the ship reported "fair weather and no problems." Then the ship with 309 men aboard was never heard from or seen again.

Three years later, a strange sight was reported off the coast of North Carolina. An old sailing ship called the *Carroll A. Deering* was bobbing around under full sail. A storm blew in and four days passed before rescuers could board the battered vessel. Everything looked normal, but the only living creatures on board were two cats. No clues revealed why the crew had deserted the ship. The full sails hinted that the weather had been good, so why would the sailors leave?

These examples of calamities to ships and airplanes in the Bermuda Triangle raise questions: Why? How? What happened?

Some of those who answer are people mystified by past events, and some are people who believe reasonable answers exist. Skeptics sneer at those who blame supernatural forces. Both sides agree that there are natural dangers in the region.

Sudden fierce squalls and rough seas are common here. Ocean whirlpools called eddies can quickly pull ships to a watery grave. A spinning waterspout—like a tornado over water—can destroy a vessel in its path.

The ocean floor of the Bermuda Triangle varies from shallow shoals to some of the deepest marine trenches in the world. Add the treacherous currents of the Gulf Stream to all of these conditions and you have a hazardous area for navigation.

But what about airplanes? The environment offers perils for them, too. Scientists are still learning about the effects of microbursts. These are powerful downdrafts that create wind shears wicked enough to demolish an airplane.

The white foamy ocean surface reported in the past could spell trouble for airplanes. Earthquake tremors can cause pockets of methane gas to escape from the ocean floor. The gas bubbles burst through churning foamy waters. A large volume of gas soaring toward an unsuspecting, low-flying aircraft might result in a stalled engine.

So what did the Christopher Columbus voyagers see in the sky? Their report of an overhead fiery streak could have been a simple meteor sighting. What about instruments showing crazy readings? Is that normal? Yes, reply some people—it's common in this section of the Atlantic Ocean. The Bermuda Triangle is a place where a compass points toward *true* north instead of the common reading of *magnetic* north. This compass variation can confuse navigators.

The skeptics also have explanations for ghostly ships whose crews evaporate without a trace. They say that sudden violent weather could make a frightened crew leave a ship in lifeboats. Then, ironically, the unoccupied ship survives the turbulent weather, but the lifeboats sink.

The scoffers maintain the disasters are merely due to a combination of natural forces: environmental conditions, equipment failures, and plain old human error. They think gossipers jump to conclusions without investigating all of the facts. Therefore, they say, the Bermuda Triangle's reputation feeds itself as each event is blown out of proportion.

Not everyone is satisfied with the answers given for each incident. These people insist the Bermuda Triangle claims far too many victims in strange ways. A wide range of theories have been put forward. Some blame aliens from outer space. Others believe there are simply unknown forces at work in the territory.

Until everyone is convinced that the accidents are due to natural causes, the Bermuda Triangle will continue to draw attention when strange things happen. Each incident will be examined and debated. Some souls will venture through the area without hesitation. Others will detour around what they believe to be risky ocean waters. After all, it's hard to change a bad reputation.

4
What Do You Feed a Carnivorous (Meat-Eating) Plant?

The guide's razor-sharp machete hacked through the tangle of vines. A small group of people trudged single file behind the guide. At the end of the line a young girl glanced around and gasped softly. Her eyes widened at the sight of an enormous plant.

Unnoticed by the others, the girl left the trail and staggered through the undergrowth toward the odd sight. Long spikes jutted from the borders of the huge green leaves. The insides of the leaves were lined with a bright red color, glistening with nectar.

Curious, the girl tiptoed close to a big leaf to examine the shiny nectar. The plant's clamshell-shaped leaves were as tall as the girl. She brushed against nearly invisible trigger hairs. Snap! Instantly the two lobes of the leaf slammed together, forming a cage. The shocked girl was trapped inside the gigantic leaf by its fringe of overlapping spikes. The steel-like jaws of the plant clamped tighter. The plant, a Venus flytrap, prepared to digest its human meal.

Do these killer plants exist? Do they really eat people? Yes and no. They exist, but on a much smaller scale. Monstrous people-eating plants appear only in science fiction stories or movies. They provide scary jungle-horror scenes.

Lucky for us, carnivorous plants don't grow big enough to munch people. Small victims, though, must watch out! A normal-sized Venus flytrap, with three- or four-inch leaves, snares and dines on little critters like insects.

Plants are usually at the bottom of the food chain. Animals chomp plants, not vice-versa. If some plants do eat meat, is this the REVENGE OF THE PLANTS?

Actually, their fondness for meat is simply because of their need for nitrogen. Meat-eating plants grow in wetlands like swamps and marshes. Soggy soil doesn't provide this important mineral, so the plants have developed a unique way of getting their doses of nitrogen—from the bodies of creatures they kill.

Since plants can't chase their prey, they have to make up for it by clever methods of capture. The Venus flytrap has an active *trigger trap*. Other kinds of plants have more passive *sticky traps*, or *pitfall traps*.

Imagine that you are an insect doing what you usually do—scurrying around, looking for food. The sweet smell of nectar draws you to a sundew plant. Tall leaf tentacles of bright green and red sparkle with dew.

But, wait! Your feet are caught in the sticky liquid. Your struggles signal the plant to emit more gooey stuff to hold you while a tentacle curls around your insect body. The plant releases enzymes—digestive juices—that begin to absorb minerals (nitrogen and others) from your soft body parts. In a day or two the sundew's leaf will uncoil and release your undigested hard body parts.

A strange sight occurs when a dragonfly becomes the sundew's victim. Flying too close to a sundew, a dragonfly can be suspended in mid-flight with wings glued to the gummy droplets.

A carpet of sundew plants glittering in the sunlight invites tired migrating butterflies to stop for a drink. A cloud of butterflies lands on the sticky tentacles. Fluttering helplessly, the butterflies are anchored by their feet to the clear gluey nectar. The innocent-looking sundew plants begin their butterfly banquet.

Butterworts are another kind of sticky trap plant that makes use of the flypaper method of capture. A greasy butter-like substance coats the leaves, giving the butterwort plant its name. The fleshy yellow-green leaves cluster close to the ground. Musty-smelling oily leaves attract insects such as ants and flies. After an insect gets stuck, the edges of the leaf curl. The butterwort's digestive juices flow around the fresh treat.

You are a bug again. This time you are lured to a pitcher plant. The odd plant is shaped like a tube with a cup-like bottom. Rainwater collects in the cup. The colorful green and white pitcher plants are decorated

with purple or red veins. Bugs like you are attracted by the aroma of sweet nectar. You eagerly climb up to the pitcher's lip and begin to sip the wonderful bait.

Soon you crawl farther into the opening to find more of the yummy nectar oozing from the plant. Trouble ahead! The inside walls of the tube are slippery. As you slide downward, your skidding is stopped by fuzzy hairs on the plant's walls. The bad news is that the hairs all point one-way. You guessed it: down. You are forced to crawl downward past the hairs, only to discover that it's impossible to go back up.

Your insect-instinct causes you to keep trying until you become exhausted. Things get worse as you eventually fall into the well of water below. Your drowned body (soft parts only) will be digested by the plant. Your hard body leftovers pile up with other victims at the bottom of the pitcher.

As an imaginary insect, you and your insect pals have been tricked by sticky trap plants and pitfall trap plants. Would you have better luck with a trigger trap plant?

Besides the Venus flytrap, this category includes the unusual bladderwort. Most bladderworts grow in still water like ponds and swamps. They float in clumps just below the surface of the water. Small yellow or purple flowers bloom above the water in the summer. Underwater, thin stems bear leaves which are actually air bags, or bladders. These bladders are tiny, growing less than one-quarter inch long. At the end of each bladder is a trapdoor that swings inward.

Small water insects are caught by suction. First the bladderwort's trapdoor is closed and the empty bladder is limp. An insect swims by and brushes against trigger hairs near the door. In a flash the bladder walls expand, forcing the trapdoor open. Slurp! A sucking action is created and water gushes in, carrying the insect with it. The trapdoor slams shut. The bladder-wort's digestive enzymes begin their work.

About forty species of meat-eating plants grow in North America. Over 500 kinds thrive in scattered countries throughout the world. That's a lot of plants turning the tables on animals. However, a few sneaky bugs outsmart the carnivorous pitcher plant.

One type of spider bungee-jumps into the center of the pitcher plant. The spider steals a partly digested meal of a fellow insect and then escapes on its silk lifeline. Some mosquito larvae and fly maggots have adapted to the plant's death pool. Immune to the pitcher's digestive juices, these larvae and maggots feed on rotted remains of trapped prey. Another insect that annoys the pitcher plant is a moth that nibbles the sugary walls of the plant. Somehow the moth clings to the slippery surfaces. Smartly walking backwards, the moth doesn't have to turn around to stroll back up the pitcher's walls.

Even birds sometimes pester the pitcher plant. Sharp beaks slit the walls of the plant. The exposed mass of insects jammed in the cup provides a feast for the birds.

None of the carnivorous plants grow into monster plants that are large enough to eat people. However, a few super-sized plants have appetites for tasty food items bigger than insects.

Found in Africa, a giant type of sundew has leaves

measuring up to two feet long. They grip and digest animals the size of mice. In tropical rainforests, a cousin of the ordinary pitcher plant grows big enough to drown and devour frogs, rats, and birds. Small monkeys have also tumbled into the pitcher's drowning pool.

These animals are the exceptions because most carnivorous plants favor a diet of small things like flies, bees, ants, grasshoppers, and spiders.

Digestion takes from a few minutes to a couple of weeks, depending on the sizes of the plant and the prey. It is not an advantage for a carnivorous plant to trap a creature larger than it can digest. The plant can die if it tries to consume an overweight victim.

Humans represent the biggest dangers to carnivorous plants. People gather large numbers of the colorful plants for bouquets. Recent protective laws should save the popular Venus flytraps from appearing in floral arrangements. Other species are not yet protected.

Most threatening to the meat-eating plants is the continuing demand for new building lands. Marshy areas where the plants thrive are shrinking. Each year people drain thousands of acres of wetlands to make way for new roads, houses, or other developments.

The good news is that many people grow carnivorous plants in greenhouses, as a hobby. Some kinds are easily grown as houseplants, such as the Venus flytrap. The Venus flytrap is happy when planted in a pot of sphagnum, a moss rich in nutrients. Besides water, it enjoys an occasional insect, for its nitrogen. The Venus flytrap is grateful to spend time outdoors, in mild weather, so it can trap a bug now and then. Some people are tempted to toss the plant a morsel of meat, but this will cause the leaves to rot. Small insects are best. The popularity of indoor-growing ensures that the fascinating plants will not completely disappear.

But will natural habitats exist in years to come? Or will carnivorous plants in the wild be wiped out? Can we let this happen? As with many similar questions about our environment, the answers depend on us.

5
What Are
Feral Children?

If you had been lost in the woods as a young toddler, could you have survived? What if a wolf heard you crying and came to investigate? After the wolf sniffed you all over she realized your helplessness and licked your face. You stopped crying, responding to this warm furry creature. The wolf was going to make a meal of you for her young cubs, but mothering instincts triggered her next reaction. She gingerly carried you to her cozy den nearby. You've been adopted.

"Feral" is defined as "wild or untamed." A feral child is one who lives alone in the wilderness, or is raised by wild animals. Tales of feral children have circulated for a long time. An ancient myth told the story of the founders of Rome, Romulus and Remus. They were rescued from the wilderness by a mother wolf. Mowgli, of Rudyard Kipling's *The Jungle Book*, was raised by wolves. Disney's movie version keeps this story alive. American folklore gave us Pecos Bill. The baby Pecos Bill fell out of a covered wagon while traveling west with his parents. He was adopted by a family of coyotes.

In recent years we've had the story of Tarzan the ape-man recycled in books, movies, and television. In the 1970s, a television series called *Lucan* focused on the unusual powers of a young man who spent his early years in a wolf den.

All fantasies? Yes, but they show our fascination with the idea of animals caring for helpless humans. Could it happen in real life? *Has* it happened?

Several cases of feral children have been written about, over the years. Some of the children survived alone, others supposedly lived with wild animals.

Way back in 1344 a story spread about a seven-year-old wolf-child who was discovered in Hesse (Germany), after spending four years in the forests. When first spotted, the boy ran on all fours and was protected by wolves.

In Lithuania, in 1694, a ten-year-old child was found living with bears. The boy spoke only with guttural sounds and walked on all fours. Back in civilization, he learned to walk upright, but he hated wearing clothes. Raw meat was his favorite food. His body was covered with scars thought to have been caused by bears.

A nine-year-old girl turned up in a small French village in 1731. Astonished villagers watched her scamper up a tree and swing from branch to branch. The girl could swim, dive, and catch frogs and fish—which she promptly ate raw. Villagers named the girl Mademoiselle LeBlanc (Miss White).

In the late 1700s another girl was found in the forests of the French Pyrenees mountains. She was identified as a sixteen-year-old who had been missing for eight years after becoming lost in a snowstorm. The teenager could no longer speak and would not eat anything but plants. She was taken to an orphanage where she remained quiet and sad, sitting with her head in her hands.

In these last two cases there was no mention of animals raising the girls, but people wondered how each one had survived the harsh wilderness with its dangers.

The "Wild Boy of Aveyron" was the first feral child case that was supported with written records. The boy was later named Victor.

In the year 1800, when he was about twelve years old, Victor was captured in a village in southern France. Because he had been sighted five years before his capture, people knew Victor had lived in the woods for a long time.

Science had now advanced so that interest in Victor was high. Scientists were eager to study this child who had lived away from civilization. They wanted to know how much influence a person's environment has on him or her. Victor was the ideal specimen for this study.

Victor's body bore many scars. A long scar on his neck looked as if someone had tried to cut his throat. He didn't walk, he trotted. He could hear, smell, and taste, but was indifferent to hot and cold. He didn't respond to speech at all. Victor's vacant eyes wandered from object to object, not stopping to focus on any one thing. He spent much of his time holding his knees while rocking back and forth.

His teacher, Jean-Marc-Gaspard Itard, wrote about the five years he worked closely with Victor. Itard hoped to teach the boy and make him "normal." After five years, Itard was disappointed that he could not achieve this even though much progress was made.

One discovery was especially important. Itard found that when a person grows up in isolation, many critical steps in development are missed. There is an ideal time for a child to learn things, such as speech, during the early years of life. If this time passes without that learning taking place, the chance for it might be lost forever.

Victor's odd life changed educational practices. The detailed notes that his teacher kept inspired others to find the best ways to help students individually. Itard's lessons were used to teach deaf children to speak. Other methods helped teach mentally challenged children.

Victor eventually was able to do simple chores. However, he was never able to talk or live a normal life. The French government paid a woman to take care of Victor until he died in 1828 when he was about forty.

Shortly after this, in 1835, a strange wolf-child story began in the Devil's River area of Texas. Mollie Dent was about to have a baby. Her frantic husband left her at their camp while he rushed to a ranch for help. After telling the ranchers about his wife, Mollie's husband was killed in a freak accident—struck by lightning while saddling his horse.

By the time the ranchers found the campsite, Mollie was dead. She had died while giving birth, but there was no trace of the baby. From lots of paw prints in the area, the ranchers concluded that wolves had devoured the infant. That seemed to be the final chapter of this young family's tragic story.

Ten years later, a boy living in the area claimed he saw a pack of wolves attacking a herd of goats. To his amazement, the boy noticed that one of the wolves was not a wolf at all. It was a naked girl crusted with dirt. Long tangles of hair fell over most of her face and body. The boy startled the pack and the girl raced away on all fours with the wolves. Months later, another sighting of the girl was reported.

Some people remembered Mollie Dent's newborn baby. Could this be the child that had disappeared ten years ago? They wondered if a female wolf had carried the infant back to her den and raised the baby with her own cubs. Several men organized a hunting party to capture the "Wolf-Girl of Devil's River."

After a three-day hunt they cornered the girl. Hissing and spitting, she bit and clawed the men as they tied her with a rope. Suddenly, a snarling wolf appeared and lunged at the men. When the wolf was killed, the shocked girl went limp.

The group stopped for the night at a nearby ranch. They locked the wolf-girl in a room with a boarded-up window. No one slept much that night. The girl yowled with loud sounds that were answered by wolves howling in the distance. As the wolves approached, the men bolted from the house, firing guns at the pack. Silently the wolves retreated into the darkness. The men discovered, to their dismay, that the girl had escaped during the frenzy. She rejoined her wolf family, and was never again seen by humans.

Like so many feral child stories, there is no proof that this story is true. It has been told and retold so many times that it's considered by many people to be nothing but a folktale.

The country of India provides several stories of children raised by wolves. Villagers often live next to thick jungles where humans and wild animals share neighborhoods. Some of the tales are obvious exaggerations, but one incident was written about with photos for evidence.

An Indian missionary by the name of J.A.L. Singh

told of an event in 1920. Two small girls, ages eight and two, were found in a wolf den. A female wolf was killed trying to protect the girls as they were being captured. The children were taken to an orphanage run by Rev. Singh and his wife.

The older girl was given the name Kamala and the two-year-old was called Amala. Both girls ate from their plates like dogs. They had to be watched carefully or they would eat dead birds and other small animals found on the ground. They walked on all fours and preferred staying awake at night. Sometimes they cried out with a wolf-sounding howl, sending shivers down the backs of those around them.

Toward the end of their first year of capture the girls became ill. A few days later little Amala died. For the first time, the older girl, Kamala, shed tears.

Although she never learned to speak in sentences, Kamala did learn to say the names of a few people and objects. Her food was placed higher and higher until Kamala learned to stand to eat and then walk upright for short distances. After another illness, Kamala's short life ended when she was about sixteen.

Rev. Singh did not write about Amala and Kamala until after both girls' deaths. Investigators did not try to verify the facts until several more years passed. By then, witnesses could not be found to back up the claims made in Rev. Singh's account.

A more recent feral child case was investigated in

the mid-1970s. In the African republic of Burundi, an eight-year-old boy was found. He became known as the "Wild Boy of Burundi." Newspaper articles told how he was found living with monkeys. The boy was cared for at an orphanage and was given the name John.

Not since Victor's case in the early 1800s had there been an opportunity like this to learn about a feral child. Two college professors from the United States traveled to Burundi to study John. After many tests, interviews, and searches for records, the two Americans solved the mystery.

John had not lived with monkeys at all. Both of his parents had died during John's first year. At age two a high fever left John with brain damage. He was moved from one orphanage to another and his records were lost. With no name and no parents, his life was a big question mark. Unable to talk, John's actions and chattering noises led to the story of his living with monkeys.

So have feral children really existed? Yes, living alone in the wilderness as Victor did. Have feral children been adopted by animals? No proof exists. The stories are captivating, but we need more evidence before accepting them as true.

Fact and fiction are hard to separate when there is no way to verify what really happened. No one investigated the truth in most of these stories while the witnesses were alive. In some cases, partial truths might have been exaggerated to add interest or amaze listeners.

Since feral children don't talk, they can't reveal what happened to them. Even if feral children learned to talk, they might not remember anything of their past in the wild. Some scientists believe that there is no memory without language.

People who study human behavior think that in some cases the feral children were *autistic*. Severely autistic children tend to have little interest in other people and can act younger than their ages. Children abandoned or lost might have been autistic before they were on their own, or the shock of being alone could have led to similar symptoms.

Some children with certain mental disorders, who have never lived alone, behave like feral children. They don't talk, they prefer to sleep in the daytime, and they bite and scratch anyone who comes close to them.

Other people counter this argument by pointing out that feral children could not have survived alone with severe mental problems. Their survival success would have taken unique abilities.

It's frightening to think of being abandoned or lost as a young child. Yet, maybe feral children intrigue us because of our fanciful notion of how it would be to live close to Mother Nature. We daydream about being truly free to do as we please, not curbed by society. The reality is that Mother Nature often lashes out with no mercy.

The dreadful physical conditions of feral children prove that their lives in the wilderness were very hard. Some of the children had parasites, like round worms, in their intestines. In all cases the children were thin and small for their ages. Their dirt-coated skin was blemished by scars and callouses. Smelly, matted tangles of hair had to be shaved.

Cut off from civilization, the children were more like wild animals than human beings. The demands of civilization may be a small price to pay for having enough food, clothing, and shelter.

We share our world with countless animals, and we feel a special kinship with them. We wonder what makes humans unique. Learning about feral children reflects the awareness that wild animals and humans are sometimes separated by a very fine line indeed.

6
Why Do Treasure Hunters Keep Digging Up Oak Island?

The men on the tall ship took a last look at the tiny island. After laboring there for weeks, their jobs were done. No one could uncover the treasure they'd hidden here. Clever tunnels and traps would keep the valuable goods safe because only a few of the men knew the code for the island's underground maze.

Once again the island was deserted as the ship melted into the distant horizon of the Atlantic Ocean. The priceless treasure rested deep in the earth.

Did this event really happen? Maybe. A scene similar to this may have occurred hundreds of years ago on a peanut-shaped island known today as Oak Island. It sits close to the coast of Nova Scotia, an eastern province of Canada. Oak Island is small—only a mile long and less than a half-mile wide at the widest point.

No one paid much attention to the island until two hundred years ago. Then Oak Island was changed by two words—BURIED TREASURE.

Most of us are excited by the idea of finding buried treasure. Visions of opening a chest crammed with shiny gold coins and glittering jewels can bring on an attack of treasure-hunting fever. We dream of instant wealth with little effort or work. It's usually not that easy. Oak Island is proof of that.

In the summer of 1795, a teenager named Daniel McGinnis rowed out to the quiet island to do some exploring. Daniel hiked through the woods and climbed a small hill. Stopping at a big oak tree, he looked up. Fifteen feet above the ground was a strange sight. A thick sawed-off limb stuck out from the trunk of the oak tree. Daniel noticed the ground beneath the short limb had settled like a shallow bowl. No one had ever lived here—so who did this?

Excitement stirred inside Daniel. Pirates had cruised these waters a hundred years earlier, and Captain Kidd was rumored to have buried treasure in the Nova Scotia area. Could this be the place? Daniel hurried back to the mainland.

The next day two friends returned with Daniel to Oak Island. They carried shovels and pickaxes. The three young men dug only 2 feet before hitting a layer of flagstones. Jackpot? Hardly. When the slabs of stone were removed, the boys saw a circular shaft 12 feet in diameter. The dirt-filled shaft's clay walls were scarred with pickaxe marks. Daniel and his friends figured that whoever created this shaft had used the sawed-off tree limb to attach hoist ropes and haul buckets of dirt out of the hole. They had probably buried a treasure and then re-filled the hole with loose dirt, the boys supposed.

Day after day the young men returned to the wide pit. They dug 10 feet down and struck a platform-like structure built of oak logs. Prying the rotted logs out of the shaft, they kept digging. Ten feet later another wooden platform was exposed. Again at 30 feet more logs appeared.

Discouraged, the three friends gave up. They needed help, so they told others about their discovery of the mysterious pit. Volunteers were scarce, as the island was believed to be haunted.

Eight years passed. Then, in 1803, a group of twenty-five men formed a company to help the three discoverers attack the shaft again.

As before, the group found oak platforms every 10 feet. They also uncovered layers of charcoal, putty, and coconut matting. Finding the coarse fiber matting excited the men. The nearest palm tree was more than 1,000 miles south. Ships, however, used coconut matting as packing for cargo. The men kept shoveling.

At a depth of 90 feet the diggers' shovels clanged on something hard. They uncovered a large flat stone carved with strange symbols, similar to hieroglyphics. The most popular story claims that the inscription was translated to read, "Forty feet below, two million pounds are buried."

The stone was found at the end of a long day of

work. Before leaving the island, the workers removed the stone. One man stuck a crowbar into the mushy dirt below and struck something firm. Was it a treasure chest? Thrilled, but too tired to work longer, the men climbed out of the deep pit. Tomorrow would be a big event.

Next morning, expecting to solve the mystery at last, the men stared, dumbfounded. The shaft was filled with seawater—at least 60 feet deep.

The flat stone they had removed worked as a seal for some kind of airlock. Disturbing the stone had allowed water to flood the deep pit. No one knew how to get rid of the water. When they tried to drain it out, bucketful by bucketful, more water gushed into the shaft. The disappointed group was defeated, and soon disbanded.

Others took their place. By 1867, eleven shafts and hundreds of feet of tunneling had been added to the original pit. Enthusiastic treasure hunters scrambled to Oak Island, then wandered away empty-handed. It became known as the Money Pit. Lots of money was going into the pit. Nothing was coming out.

During the 1800s, one group's luck seemed promising. Using a mining bit, they drilled down 98 feet, burrowing through wood, metal, and then wood again. Could it be a wooden chest? The bit was brought up. Attached to it were three small gold chain links—more tantalizing objects, but nothing of real value. This group ran out of patience *and* money.

For the next one hundred years, the earth gave up just enough objects to keep fortune hunters flocking to the island. Here's what was found:

- An ivory whistle
- A piece of parchment with the inked letters "V" and "I"
- Bits of iron and brass
- Samples of wood carbon-dated to the year 1575
- More coconut fiber matting—lots of it

By the 1900s, an important item from the early dig had disappeared—the large flat stone with the carved symbols. The gold links vanished, too. Critics wonder if the objects had ever existed.

What do believers think is buried on Oak Island? One theory is that Oak Island was used like a bank by pirates. The Money Pit and underground tunnels act as a decoy. Each group of pirates dug tunnels off the main shaft. After carefully mapping the area, loot could be retrieved by simply digging straight down from above.

Adding weight to this proposal is a curious looking heart-shaped stone found on Oak Island. Similar stones turned up in pirate banks on Haiti, an island in the Caribbean Sea. Skeptics say pirates would not have been organized enough to build the complicated tunnels.

Some people wonder if the treasure belonged to the Vikings. Others speak of British ships prowling the nearby waters during the Revolutionary War. This leads people to think British soldiers landed on Oak Island to stash funds that had been sent to them from England.

Or perhaps the treasure was gold stolen from the Aztecs or Incas. A popular tale describes a Spanish ship packed with treasures looted from the New World. The Gulf Stream carried the ship to Nova Scotia where the crew unloaded the heavy valuables and stored them underground. As the story goes, on the voyage back to Spain, the ship sank. No survivors meant that Oak Island's secrets were protected.

It took years for treasure hunters to figure out some of the island's mysteries. The shaft was booby-trapped with a system of horizontal tunnels and stone-lined drain channels. The rising tide poured ocean water into the tunnels, filling the lower part of the Money Pit. Though frustrated by the elaborate underground system, searchers admired the skills it took to construct it.

Frustrations didn't keep people from trying, though. In 1909 a future United States president, Franklin D. Roosevelt, bought stock in one treasure-seeking company. At the time Roosevelt was a young law clerk. Like many others, he was fascinated by Oak Island's challenge.

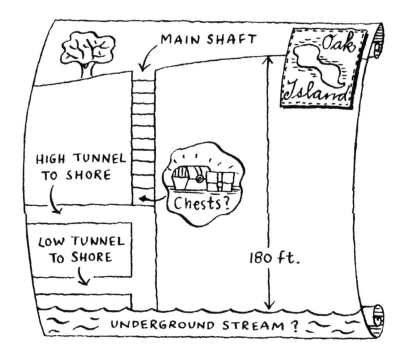

In the 1930s, a group tackled the project with a steam shovel. It failed. Another drilling crew tried their luck. Nothing. By now the island looked like an active minefield with holes, tunnels, and piles of dirt everywhere. The place was beginning to resemble the site of a groundhog convention.

One hopeful hunter, Dan Blankenship, moved to Oak Island in 1969. Dan's voice tingles with excitement when he talks about a 230-foot shaft that he drilled, called Borehole 10-X. In 1971, Blankenship watched a monitor of a closed-circuit underwater camera located at the bottom of the deep shaft. As Dan stared at the monitor, he claimed to see the bones of a severed human hand float across the screen. He also viewed the outline of wooden boxes and tools. Photos of the camera's tape show dark shadows and murky outlines. Most people were unable to see what Dan saw in the fuzzy pictures.

But Dan is convinced there's treasure to be found. He believes the entire island is filled with clues. This view is shared by another long time resident, Fred Nolan. Dan and Fred claim they found stones and other markers like a drilled rock, a boulder pierced with a steel ring, and several old wooden stakes.

Some of the treasure hunts have ended in tragedy. A total of six people have died on the island. The worst accident happened in the mid-1960s. Four men drowned in shallow water at the bottom of a 27 foot shaft. Before drowning, they had passed out from fumes given off by a pump they were using.

Over the years, about two million dollars have been spent trying to recover the treasure. Untold man hours have been logged. Oak Island has been overrun by professional engineers and geologists, as well as swarms of amateurs. They have used construction equipment, pumps, compressors, drills, even dynamite.

The big question is: WHY HAS NOTHING OF VALUE BEEN FOUND?

Could it be that a treasure was found in past years—maybe by one person or a group sworn to secrecy? They might have wanted to avoid paying a royalty or tax to the government of Nova Scotia. Or, did the original designers of the Money Pit return and remove the valuables? Was a treasure ever left on the island in the first place? Perhaps the tunnels were used to temporarily store something else.

If the treasure is still there, maybe it has dropped or shifted to a new position. This is possible due to underlying limestone carved with cavities and sinkholes. Drilling could have broken up wooden chests, scattering the treasure.

Negative thoughts like these haven't stopped the army of hopeful hunters who have invaded Oak Island for 200 years. All were rewarded with only shattered dreams.

But, treasure-hunting frenzy has never been in short supply. Human nature leads us to dream of winning the lottery. Becoming instantly rich is a popular fantasy. For some people, treasure-seeking is a sport where they can match wits with the treasure-hiders. So it's no surprise that the hunt continues.

A recent venture is a group called the Triton Alliance. It is a private company of American and Canadian investors raising ten million dollars. They are sinking a huge concrete shaft down through the original Money Pit. The concrete shaft is massive—80 feet wide and 200 feet deep. Triton is determined to settle the treasure question once and for all. If the group is successful, it will become worldwide news.

As long as no big treasure is unearthed, the strange saga of Oak Island quietly goes on,

and on,

and on . . .

7
Who's Afraid
of Voodoo and Zombies?

What image appears when we think of *voodoo*? We probably imagine someone sticking pins into a doll-like figure. The doll looks like and represents a real person. The pins are supposed to cause the real person pain. Or bad luck suddenly strikes. The holder of the doll grins wickedly, knowing that the pins are harming the victim.

Now what image appears when we think of *zombies*? We can thank scary movies for these images. Zombies rise from their graves at night. They stagger through the darkness, searching for victims. The zombies are dressed in moldy burial clothes that hang like rags. Bones show through their rotted skin. Most frightening of all are their faces—no expressions and blank staring eyes. The grotesque flesh-eaters return to the cemetery before daylight. They are the walking dead, the creatures of our worst nightmares that cause us to wake up screaming.

Hollywood gave us this gory, supernatural monster-zombie. But that's not the voodoo version where the zombie legend actually began.

The history of zombies is not easy to track because voodoo is a religion, and it is complicated. Unlike other religions, voodoo has no formal school of training for the priesthood, and has no written doctrine. Because of this, voodooism has constantly changed over the years. At the same time there are some widely held beliefs.

Voodoo's roots are in Africa. The word *voodoo* means "spirit," and came from West Africa. More than 300 years ago the voodoo religion sprouted in the Caribbean island of Haiti after African slaves were brought to the New World. The slaves came from different parts of Africa and held a wide variety of religious beliefs.

Slaves arriving in Haiti were forced by their French masters to practice the Catholic religion. Over the years the slaves blended Catholicism with the religions brought from Africa. Adding to the mix was the influence of mysterious secret rituals, magic, and belief in the supernatural.

By the 1790s elaborate ceremonies were being performed using live snakes. A supernatural being was represented by the serpent. This all-powerful god was a god of goodness. Under the serpent god in importance were the *loa* (lesser gods). The loa were identified with the saints of the Catholic Church, but given African names.

Early voodooism became a cult of rebellion. In the

late 1700s leaders of slave revolts in Haiti used voodoo ceremonies to inflame their followers.

By the early 1800s, several thousand refugees from Haiti had arrived in the United States. They had escaped from the bloody struggles for power taking place in Haiti. Most of the refugees settled in New Orleans, Louisiana. Voodoo influences are still found in New Orleans. Its popularity in the United States is quite mild, though, compared to that in Haiti. Voodooism thrives in the small Caribbean island.

In Haiti today, many of the people attend Catholic Church services on Sundays. God is the Supreme Being and Christian rituals are followed. During other days of the week, however, voodoo is the popular religion for most Haitians.

A voodoo priest is called a *houngan*. Women often play a major role in voodooism. A priestess is called a *mambo*. The priest or priestess conducts ceremonies and performs animal sacrifices.

A voodoo religious ceremony can be thrilling to watch. The air is filled with the heavy aroma of incense. A fire burns in front of the altar. Drums beat, dancers sway to the pounding rhythm. The beat throbs louder, faster, faster. A few swirling dancers seem to be possessed by spirits. They fall into a trance with their bodies jerking. Several dancers lift glowing embers from the fire and lick them with their tongues.

They are unharmed by the red hot embers. The frenzied drumming slows. Exhausted dancers collapse.

A mambo dressed in a gown of red, gold, and white approaches the altar. Prayers are offered. To a quiet steady drumbeat the priestess raises a chicken toward the sky, up and down three times. With one sharp knife stroke the priestess cuts the chicken's throat. The animal is offered to the loa as a tribute.

Watching a voodoo ceremony, as an outsider, is like peering through a curtained window guarded by mysterious sentries. You see something through the glass, but maybe it is only what you are *allowed* to see.

For everyday living, a houngan or mambo makes and sells charms of all kinds. If you wish a person ill, you can buy a voodoo doll charm fashioned of feathers and wound with black thread. Each day some of the thread is unwound and the feathers slowly fall off. This is supposed to cause bad things to happen to the intended victim.

Good deed charms are popular, too. The houngan or mambo provides charms for winning someone's love. Other charms bring luck or protect against evil omens. There are even charms for undoing tricks— breaking the hex (bad spell) someone has put on you.

Some priests or priestesses are called "leaf doctors." Skilled in herbal medicine, they cure simple sicknesses such as headaches, stomachaches, and fevers.

This is a valuable service to people due to the shortage of medical doctors, and the poverty in Haiti.

For Haitians, life after death is a complex belief. When a person dies, believers in voodoo think that part of the person's soul or spirit stays with the family. Greatly respected ancestors can join the loa, and their spirits are then honored by both family members and others. This ancestor worship has a background in countries around the world as well as in Africa.

A voodooist has unusual beliefs when it comes to the dead body itself. The corpse, empty of its soul, can be stolen and used again. This is where zombies come in.

It is believed, by some, that a dead body can be turned into a zombie by a *bokor*, a person who practices sorcery and black magic. To protect their dead from becoming zombies, family members keep watch over their loved ones for the first few days after death.

For zombie-making, the bokor needs the help of the god of death, Baron Samedi. Also known as the "Lord of the Graveyard," Baron Samedi's symbol is the skull and crossbones, commonly seen in Haitian cemeteries. The baron is described as looking like an undertaker. He carries a walking stick and wears a long black coat and a bowler hat. The baron controls zombies.

Standing over a newly dead corpse, the bokor utters secret chants to Baron Samedi. Then he mixes magic potions to bring life back into the dead body. Unlike

the movie-zombies that are always evil, the zombie of voodooism is merely a robot obeying its master's commands. It is now under the control of the bokor. The zombie has life but no longer has a soul or a mind of its own. And it does *not* devour people like the movie-zombie. Haitians are not afraid of being harmed by a zombie, but they have great fear of being *turned into* a zombie.

This occasional demonstration of zombie-making is how some bokors hold power over their followers. Although many lively tales of zombies circulate, not much evidence backs them up. No one has ever proved that a zombie existed, but the legend continues.

It is not clear how or why the zombie legend started. In some stories, zombies are treated like slaves—even beaten. People compare the actions of zombies to real slaves of the past. In order to escape punishment and survive, some slaves had to act like robots. Maybe slaves invented the zombie stories simply to scare their masters. Or perhaps power-hungry leaders used zombie tales to threaten and control their followers.

Another theory is that zombie lore arose to describe living people with severe mental problems. Since little has been understood about mental illness in the past, it could have led to superstitious beliefs.

In some cases today, a bokor with a knowledge of drugs might give potions to a living person who only appears to die. Breathing and heartbeats are so faint that the person is declared dead. Later the bokor feeds the "dead" person a brew that revives him, but causes a state of confusion. The dazed person behaves like a zombie, doing what the bokor commands.

Medical doctors who examined three cases of alleged zombies in Haiti in 1997 wrote about their findings. All three of the people were diagnosed by the doctors as having mental illnesses. They were not zombies.

The same doctors interviewed two bokors. Both sorcerers admitted to having used poisonous drugs for zombie-making. The life they created from death was only an illusion.

Many Haitians are sensitive about the views outsiders have of the voodoo religion. Rightly so. The openness and sharing of voodoo ceremonies is often rewarded with bad publicity.

Voodoo superstitions coated in mystery are targets for mud-slingers. Many types of rituals exist in the religion, but most outside interest spotlights the gore. Voodooism is attacked for its bloody animal sacrifices. And, exaggerations about zombies add to the negative views.

Outsiders tend to criticize what they don't understand—and voodoo is not an easy religion to understand. However, it is colorful, puzzling, and complicated—yet endlessly fascinating.

8
Do Mermaids Exist?

Local people spotted the mermaid bobbing in the waves offshore. One person threw rocks at her. A few days later the mermaid's lifeless body washed up on the beach. The year was 1830 and the event happened on the island of Benbecula, northwest of Scotland.

Years later, a writer interviewed people who saw or touched the mermaid. They said she had "the upper body of a very small woman. Her smooth skin was white and she had long dark hair. The lower part of her body was like a salmon, but without scales."

The island's sheriff was convinced she was part human. He covered the mermaid with a shroud and buried her in a small coffin.

Three years passed. Then six Scottish fishermen claimed they caught a similar creature in their nets. The mermaid cried and howled for hours until the frazzled fishermen released her back into the sea.

Worldwide folklore tells about strange creatures that look human from head to waist. But from the waist down they possess tails like fish. Most stories describe beautiful mermaids who sit on rocks. They comb their long hair and admire themselves in hand-held mirrors. When a rare male of the species—a mer-man—appears in a story, he is usually portrayed as being ugly.

Mermaid stories around the world share some common features. Mermaids:

- cannot stay out of the water for long
- will eventually smother in the air like a fish out of water
- will, if kept in a pool, miss the open sea so much that they will weaken and wither away

In earliest history, the half-human, half-fish beings were shown in carvings and statues as gods and goddesses of the waters. Mermaids and mermen appeared in Babylonian art and myths as early as 5,000 B.C.

One mermaid tale began in ancient Greece. In Greek mythology, Sirens were lovely women with the lower bodies of birds. Around 300 B.C. the image of the Sirens changed. Now they had tails like fish, so they became mermaids. The cruel Sirens swam near treacherous rocks, singing enchanting songs. Sailors could not resist the music and were lured to their doom, crashing their ships against the rocks.

A famous Greek myth tells about a ship captain, Odysseus, who finds a way to resist the temptations of the Sirens. Odysseus orders his crew members to tie him to a mast. Then he has the crew stuff their ears with wax. Soon Odysseus hears the mystical music. He sobs and screams to be set free so he can fling himself into the sea. Unable to hear his pleas, Odysseus's crew sails the vessel safely past the bewitching Sirens.

The Sirens in the myths are the origin for the present use of the word, *siren*, as a warning of danger. Today the high-pitched wail of a siren warns us of emergencies.

Over the years, sightings of real mermaids have been announced. During his 1492 voyage to America, Christopher Columbus and some of his sailors spied three mermaids. Columbus wrote that "they were not as beautiful as they are painted, although to some extent they have a human appearance in the face. . . ." He also noted that the crew observed similar creatures on an earlier voyage near West Africa.

Another explorer, an English navigator named Henry Hudson, wrote in his journal about a mermaid incident in 1608. Two of his crew members declared, "from the navel upward . . . she was like a woman . . . her body as big as one of us; her skin white; and long hair hanging down of color black; in her going down we saw her tail which was like the tail of a porpoise, and speckled like a mackerel." The two sailors claimed they noticed the mermaid while sailing on Hudson's ship near a group of islands off northern Russia.

Occasional sightings continued throughout the

years. In the 1800s, public interest in mermaids was high. This led to hoaxes. The famous showman P.T. Barnum exhibited what he said was a preserved mermaid. Years later, in his autobiography, Barnum confessed that the specimen was "ugly, dried-up, and black-looking . . . about three feet long." Crowds of people waited in long lines and paid to gawk at the fake mermaid.

Phony mermaids were sometimes made by hoaxers who joined together parts of different dead animals. Usually the upper half was a shaved monkey attached to the bottom half of a similar-sized fish.

Other fakes were produced by cutting, shaping and drying certain types of large fish so they resembled humans. The shriveled creatures with formed faces and arms fooled some people into believing they were part human. P.T. Barnum's quote, "There's a sucker born every minute!" reminds us that people often see only what they *want* to see.

In the mid-1980s, researchers went to Papua New Guinea. They investigated a sea creature called a *Ri* by the people there. Native witnesses claimed the Ri had a human-like head and upper torso. A scientific expedition revealed that the animal was only a dugong, a member of the sea cow family.

Some scientists think another type of sea cow, the manatee, has also been mistaken for a mermaid in the past. Like its dugong cousin, the gray manatee has an

overweight-torpedo shape. It grows to be 10 or 12 feet long. The gentle vegetarian grazes on water plants. Because it is a mammal, it glides to the surface to breathe, showing off a whiskered muzzle, cow-like lips, and large nostrils.

Some fans of the manatee think it is so homely that it is irresistibly adorable. The blunt head contains small eyes, pinholes for ears, and a thick short neck that is bigger than the head. A manatee is largest at the shoulders, where a flipper extends from each side of its belly. Aided by a broad paddle-like tail, the chubby manatee cruises smoothly through the water. Could manatees be the mermaids that Christopher Columbus wrote about? If so, when compared with mermaids he had viewed in artwork, it's not surprising that he said "they were not as beautiful as they are painted. . . ."

Besides the sea cow family, some people propose that a spy-hopping whale or walrus could account for a mermaid sighting. A spy-hopping mammal rises vertically out of the water to glance around. Seen from far away, and with some imagination, it might look like a human surfacing. And, couldn't a seal basking on rocks resemble a mermaid, if observed from a great distance?

Other people believe that mermaids could be creatures not yet known to science. There is much we do not know about the oceans that cover over 70 percent of our planet. Using submersibles, marine biologists continue to discover new life forms. Will they someday find mermaids frolicking in the dark depths of the ocean?

A famous monument in Denmark confirms our fascination with mermaids. Near the entrance to Copenhagen Harbor sits the statue of the Little Mermaid from Hans Christian Andersen's popular story. It is one of the most photographed statues in the world.

We have no proof that mermaids exist. Yet they charm and inspire our imaginations. Perhaps mermaids are simply symbols of the lure of the sea—its beauty, excitement, and temptations. At the same time, mermaids represent the sea's dangers and mysterious secrets. When gazing at the ocean, listen hard for the whispers of mermaids as the waves break on the rocky shore.

9
What's Creepier– a Scorpion or a Tarantula?

Make a choice. Enter a dark room that contains a scorpion, or go into a dark room that holds a tarantula. Is certain death awaiting you in one of the rooms?

An angry scorpion is a scary sight. The scorpion in the room might be one that grows to a paper plate-sized 8 inches long. The scorpion waves small pincers and flexes a pair of lobster-like claws, ready to grab its prey. Curved over its back is a vicious-looking tail tipped with a poisonous stinger. The scorpion sees you in the darkness. Light-sensitive eyes allow it to navigate outdoors using shadows cast by starlight.

Perhaps the tarantula is less terrifying. Then again, it could be as big as the scorpion, another eight-incher. The hairy tarantula rears up on its back pair of fuzzy legs, showing off fangs full of venom. Some species hiss when they rise, causing more fear. A tarantula's eyesight is bad, but it feels slight vibrations. When you move, the tarantula will know where you are.

The choice of dark rooms is not easy. Neither critter is likely to be voted "cuddly pet of the month." But is one more dangerous than the other? Both look ferocious, and both can deliver a sting when in the mood.

The two creatures are cousins. The tarantula is the largest member of the spider family. Scorpions and tarantulas are both arachnids. Animals in this group have two body parts and eight legs; insects have six.

Scorpions and tarantulas have in common:

Molting:	They shed hard outer bodies as they grow.
Nocturnal activity:	Active night-hunters, they are sluggish during day.
Diet:	They feast on insects like beetles, crickets, locusts, caterpillars, and grasshoppers.
Stinging:	Both paralyze victims with poisonous stinger or fangs.
Mouths:	Neither has teeth, so they suck juices from their prey.
Mating:	Females of both sometimes turn into cannibals after mating. Males run for their lives from hungry females as soon as they mate.
Life span:	Both live for a long time, compared to other animals. Some scorpions live up to twenty-five years. Some tarantulas have a life span of twelve years for a male, twenty to twenty-five years for a female.

Of the hundreds of species of scorpions, about twenty kinds live in the United States. Among these twenty, the one deadly type lives in Arizona and southern Utah. All other species in the U.S. have stings no worse than a bee. In general, the bigger a scorpion's claws, the less dangerous is its venom. The most poisonous have thin claws that are useless for grabbing and crushing. The scorpion relies on whipping its poisonous tail forward to jab a victim.

It is estimated that three to five thousand people die from scorpion stings each year. Most of these deaths occur in India, Africa, South America, and Mexico.

If you think scorpions are scary-looking, be glad some extinct varieties are no longer around. Fossils of water scorpions have been found that measured a whopping 10 feet long. And land dwellers up to 3 feet long once existed. These huge creatures lived three or four hundred million years ago. By comparison, today's scorpions are shrimp-sized, ranging from 1/2 inch to 8 inches long. Common colors are yellowish, brown, or black.

Most scorpions make their homes in warm places, burrowing underground. Others live in caves, trees, jungles, and even in high mountains. As members of the food chain, they are eaten by owls, bats, lizards, snakes, and mice. To avoid a sting, a predator might snap off the poisonous tail before munching a scorpion.

Before they mate, scorpions grab each other's claws and perform an elaborate courtship dance. After mating, the wise male scurries to safety, to avoid becoming the female's next meal.

The female does not give birth for a remarkably long time—three to eighteen months, depending on the species. Born alive, the baby scorpions climb on their mother's back and ride around for several days. Then they scramble off on their own. Many of the youngsters become food for other animals, including bigger scorpions who don't mind dining on smaller scorpions. Scorpion cannibalism is common.

Scorpions do not travel far. They like to sit and wait for food to come to them. Scientists studying scorpions have described them as being champion "couch potatoes."

When a scorpion catches and stings a food item, such as a cricket, it clutches the victim with its claws. The scorpion seems to chew on the cricket, but actually, the scorpion is injecting enzymes, or digestive juices. This turns the soft parts of the cricket into soupy liquid that the scorpion sucks into its stomach.

As night hunters, many scorpions hide in cool dark places during the day. In scorpion-friendly desert climates, people check their shoes before putting them on, in case you-know-who is napping inside.

An "old wives' tale" says that if a scorpion is surrounded by a ring of fire, it will sting itself to death, rather than burn. Not true, of course.

Another tall tale was connected to tarantulas over 300 years ago. In southern Italy, the *Lycosa tarantula* was mistakenly identified as a poisonous species whose bite was fatal. When a person was bitten by the spider, it was thought that the victim could be cured only one way. The individual had to dance a wild dance called the *tarantella*. Unfortunately, many frantic people only danced themselves to death—at least those bitten by the other type of spider that was actually deadly.

Out of 800 tarantula species, about thirty kinds live in the southwestern United States. Some of the brown or black hairy tarantulas we are familiar with grow up to five inches long. But, most of these furry spiders are small enough to fit in the palm of your hand.

Larger kinds, like the Mexican red-knee tarantula, are sold as pets. Pet owners claim their tarantulas are shy and gentle. It's not a good idea to let a pet tarantula crawl up on a person's arms or shoulders. Not because of danger to the person, but because the tarantula might tumble off. If a tarantula falls, it is easily injured or can die. It's hard to think of a monstrous spider being as fragile as glass.

Usually tarantulas will bite only what they plan to eat, and human beings are too large for their menu. If a human is bitten, the bite feels like a bee sting. The tarantula doesn't have enough venom to harm a person. However, people who are allergic to bee stings might react seriously to the spider's poison.

Larger tarantulas will attack small animals like mice. The tarantula's hollow fangs inject venom into the mouse, paralyzing it. Like the scorpion, the tarantula's mouthpiece contains digestive juices. The soft insides of the mouse are liquified. It might take more than a day for the tarantula to polish off the "mouse-shake." All that is left of the mouse is a small pile of bones and fur.

If a tarantula has a lucky day and kills extra prey, like a beetle, the big spider saves it for later. The tarantula spins silk, wraps up the beetle, and drags it back to its burrow.

Unlike other spiders, tarantulas don't live in webs. They prefer cozy burrows. Some species live in trees, but most have underground homes.

At mating time, a male tarantula finds a female's burrow. He taps on the entrance, she comes out, and they mate. Like the male scorpion, the male tarantula runs away fast, worried about becoming the female's dinner.

Soon the female tarantula spins a web pad on the floor of her burrow, preparing the nursery. She lays several hundred eggs on the web, then rolls it into a big white ball called an egg sac. The ball is blanketed by her body during cool nights. On sunny days, she shoves the ball to the burrow's entrance to warm the eggs.

In about six weeks the eggs hatch. After a few days the babies leave, scampering in all directions. Many baby tarantulas are gobbled by snakes, lizards, or other tarantulas. Survivors dig their own burrows, where they will spend most of their lives.

When threatened by a predator, a tarantula will run and hide. If the big spider can't escape, it stands up on its back legs, displaying its fangs. Sometimes the tarantula hisses a warning by rubbing its front legs together. If the enemy doesn't back off, some species of tarantulas do an odd thing. The spider uses its hind legs to break off hairs from its abdomen and throws the hairs at the attacker. Each hair has tiny hooks and barbs that can temporarily blind eyes or cause a burning itch on skin.

One enemy not intimidated by the tarantula is a type of spider wasp nicknamed a "tarantula hawk." After the female wasp mates and is ready to lay eggs, the wasp hunts for a tarantula. The female wasp waits until the big spider lifts up on its hind legs. Then the spider wasp quickly stings the tarantula in its belly. The wasp drags the paralyzed tarantula to a hole in the ground.

After laying an egg on the tarantula's body, the wasp covers the hole with dirt. Soon a newborn wasp hatches from the egg and feeds on the paralyzed, but still living, tarantula. This can go on for weeks. Finally the spider is killed by the young wasp.

Due to their looks, scorpions and tarantulas don't have a lot of fans, but the two cousins do have some good points.

Scorpions have benefited human stroke victims. Strokes are sudden attacks that can leave people paralyzed. Scientists studied the effects of scorpion venom, then developed a drug for treating strokes in humans.

Tarantulas are helpful because they eat insects that destroy green leaves and grain crops. These same good deeds also apply to scorpions, since they have an appetite for insects harmful to plants. Nature is kept in balance.

Back to the dark room. While you still might not fancy being alone with either creepy-crawler, simply knowing more about them can make you less fearful. Most of us probably would risk the tarantula's bee sting bite, rather than test our luck against a scorpion that *might* be the deadly poisonous type. Then again, why worry? Because of your size, think how frightful you must look to the scorpion or tarantula.

10

What Happened to Atlantis?

Atlantis was the ideal place to live. The huge island was lush with green plains, clear streams, birds, animals, and gardens. The capital city stood on a hill circled by three rings of water connected by canals and locks. White marble buildings topped with gold flashed in the sunlight. Temples and pyramids pointed toward the sky. Fountains bubbled with both hot and cold water. Miles of stone walls and paved roads snaked through the big island.

With their advanced skills and learning, the people of Atlantis were happy and proud of their paradise on earth. Then they became greedy, wanting more. They wanted to conquer other countries. But disaster struck, and Atlantis was wiped out.

Did it really exist or is the lost continent of Atlantis a story that just won't go away?

In an ancient Greek story, Poseidon, a god of the sea, named his first son Atlas. Both the Atlantic Ocean and the island of Atlantis were named for Atlas.

Plato, a famous Greek philosopher, lived around 400 B.C. He wrote about the beautiful rich island of

Atlantis that had disappeared many years in the past. Atlantis vanished when earthquakes shook the island and floods demolished all traces of it.

Did Plato make up this story, or did he believe it was truly a part of history? This question is still debated. Of course, there are plenty of theories to go around. Hundreds of books praise the once mighty Atlantis.

A popular book of the year 1516 was *Utopia*, by England's Sir Thomas More. Utopia is a Greek word meaning "no place." The tale is about an imaginary island where life is nearly perfect. It's the same view many people have of Atlantis.

Then, in 1624, Sir Francis Bacon stirred imaginations with *The New Atlantis*. His story described a country called Bensalem. The people of Bensalem had superhuman knowledge. They understood flight and built structures a half-mile high. Readers wondered if this was how life had been on the fabled missing continent.

In the late 1800s a former U.S. congressman, Ignatius Donnelly, rekindled interest in Atlantis. He wrote a bestseller, *Atlantis: The Antediluvian World*. *Antediluvian* means "ancient." It refers to the world as it was before the Flood as described in the Bible. Many versions of the story about the disappearance of Atlantis do refer to raging floods after a volcanic blast.

Donnelly believed Plato's account was actual history. Atlantis was the first great civilization. In fact, Donnelly thought all others sprang from it. Survivors from Atlantis migrated to different areas of the world, he claimed. Some reached the Americas, others went to Europe and Africa. In Donnelly's opinion, refugees from Atlantis were the prehistoric ancestors of the future great civilizations—the Egyptian, Greek, even the Aztec, Mayan, and Incan civilizations in the Americas.

Donnelly's viewpoint persuaded others. They noted the ways these cultures were alike, ranging from the games they played to similar artwork and styles of buildings.

Some scholars think this explains how the Spanish explorer, Cortés, defeated the Aztecs after he landed in Mexico in 1519. The Spanish soldiers numbered only around five hundred. The Aztecs, under their king, Montezuma, had tens of thousands of warriors. But in just two years the Spanish had conquered the Aztecs. How could this happen?

In ancient Aztec legends, the god Quetzalcoatl was a tall bearded white man who first appeared after a catastrophe hid the sun for a long time. Quetzalcoatl brought back the sun. He also taught the Aztecs arts of civilization. Some of the Aztecs did not trust this god and attempted to kill him. Quetzalcoatl returned to the sea, promising to return one day. Some people believe Cortés was successful because the Aztecs thought he was Quetzalcoatl.

Where did this legend start? Was this "god" from Atlantis, and did he pass on knowledge of science, mathematics, and astronomy to the emerging civilization in the Americas? It must be pointed out that many scholars laugh at this notion.

Jules Verne was another author who couldn't resist writing about Atlantis. Verne was a science fiction writer who described inventions that were many years in the future. In 1870 Verne's novel, *20,000 Leagues Under the Sea,* astonished readers. The main character, Captain Nemo, cruises in his submarine called the *Nautilus.* Among the wonders he sees are the ruins of a beautiful underwater city, the lost continent of Atlantis. Years later, this classic novel was made into a movie.

As with so many legends, books and movies keep the subject of Atlantis alive. And, throughout the world, when ocean divers find strange manmade walls or structures underwater, Atlantis's name is linked with the discovery.

Sometimes legends are proved to be true. The city of Troy was once thought to be a place in Greek mythology. The Greek poet Homer made Troy famous in his story based on ancient legend.

A long war raged between Greece and the people of Troy, the Trojans. The Greeks were unable to break into the city of Troy. Then the Greeks built a large wooden horse and left it outside the walls of the city.

The Greek troops marched away. The Trojans thought the Greeks had given up and left the horse as a peace offering. So the celebrating Trojans pulled the wooden horse inside their walls. That night, Greek soldiers who had been hiding inside the big wooden horse emerged and opened the gates of the city. Greek troops swarmed into Troy, defeating the stunned Trojans. It was a triumph in ancient warfare. "Beware of the Trojan horse" is a phrase still used to warn of hidden dangers that destroy from within.

Troy was not considered to be a real place until 1873. That's when Troy's ruins were discovered and identified, surprising many people. Atlantis's believers think a similar thing will happen when the lost continent is found someday.

Some scholars think Plato was describing a place close to Greece, in the Aegean Sea. They say his report could be based on the actual history of an island called Thera.

Scientists know that Thera's 4,900 foot volcano exploded around 1470 B.C. The violence was so great that what remains of the island is covered in a thick layer of volcanic pumice and ash. Severe earthquakes first shook the island, followed by the blast of the volcano. As the crater collapsed, the sea flooded over parts of the island. This could account for the continent that was "swallowed by the sea," as Plato wrote.

For the past thirty years, archaeologists have dug in

the hardened ash to uncover a city on Thera, which is called Santorini today. Relics of the Minoan Empire have surfaced. This advanced society had written laws and engineering skills. Suddenly the Minoan Empire vanished around the time of the volcanic eruption of 1470 B.C. The empire was centered on the island of Crete, 60 miles north. Crete and Thera together could have inspired the Atlantis story.

Not so, say critics. Plato said Atlantis was outside the "Pillars of Hercules." He was referring to the Strait of Gibraltar, they claim, so Atlantis had to be in the Atlantic Ocean.

Islands can appear and disappear in the Atlantic. On the ocean bottom in the Mid-Atlantic Ridge there is a large crack. This is blamed on the movement of the continental plates. Underwater mountains form as the magma rises from the earth's molten interior. Undersea volcanoes can give birth to new islands, as well as cause the disappearance of others. The rise and fall of land masses usually takes thousands of years, but an active volcano can speed up the process.

Here are just a few of the many theories about Atlantis:

Certain animals seem to "remember" a lost island in the mid-Atlantic. Eels from rivers in Europe and America swim to a mating spot in the middle of the Atlantic Ocean. Birds migrating from Europe to South America circle over this area of the Atlantic. They seem to be searching for a resting place that no longer exists. Lemmings leave Norway and swim out to the ocean as if looking for land that is no longer there. The confused lemmings swim in circles until they drown. In all of these cases the animals' instincts draw them toward the same mid-Atlantic region.

Around ten or eleven thousand years ago, an asteroid may have slammed into the Atlantic Ocean with the power of 30,000 hydrogen bombs. A rift stretching from Iceland to Puerto Rico opened in the ocean bottom. Most of Atlantis was pulled into the rift, resulting in earthquakes, tidal waves, and poisonous gases that blocked the sun. After the tragedy, nine small islands were left—the present Azores. These were once the nine highest peaks on Atlantis. This theory pleases those who claim that survivors of Atlantis influenced early civilizations in the Americas.

It is further believed by some people that the continent was destroyed at exactly 8 P.M. on June 5, 8498 B.C. Where did this date come from? This is when the calendar of the Maya civilization begins—their "point zero" time. That was about 10,500 years ago—close to the time Atlantis was destroyed, according to some theories.

Among those searching for an Atlantis in the Atlantic are divers who have explored underwater ruins near Bimini, in the Bahamas. In the 1940s a man named Edgar Cayce described these Bimini ruins, which were not actually found until twenty years later. Cayce was a famous clairvoyant—a person who reveals information about the future while in a trance-like sleep. Scientists on recent diving explorations do not all agree that the Bimini ruins are manmade. Some think they are merely boulders eroded by nature. The clairvoyant Cayce also said that the people of Atlantis used crystals as sources of a mysterious power. There's an interesting connection to Edgar Cayce's remark about crystals. A crystal skull was found in 1927 in an ancient city built by the Maya. It is a life-sized sculpture of a human skull carved from quartz. According to some persons who have examined it, the transparent skull glows with changing colors and emits tinkling bell sounds. These observers think the crystal skull has strange powers. That's all a few people needed to hear to link the skull's origin to Atlantis.

How can one place, Atlantis, be the springboard for such a wide range of speculation? No concrete proof has been offered for any of the theories—wild or mild as they may be.

The dreamer side of our human nature likes to imagine a perfect place to live. We try to develop a society filled with happiness for all, but our daily news broadcasts bombard us with reminders of our weaknesses.

Does Atlantis represent an ideal society that was lost, or does it stand for what we hope to attain? Does it even matter if it really existed?

Someday archaeologists may find proof there was an Atlantis. But until then, we can only wonder.

11
Do Snake Charmers Really Charm Snakes?

Near a bustling marketplace in the country of India, a man carefully places a covered basket on the ground. He unrolls a rug and sits on it cross-legged.

Removing the basket's lid, the man begins to play a small flute-like instrument. The haunting notes of the tune cause people to stop and stare. The melody becomes louder and faster. The basket jiggles. Suddenly a snake's head lunges up, looks around, then settles its piercing eyes on the flute player.

Like a sinister symbol of doom, the six-foot cobra rises, lifting the upper third of its body straight up. The ribs in its neck spread to form a broad, flat hood. The man weaves from side to side, returning the fearsome snake's icy glare. Looking for a place to strike, the serpent sways to the man's rhythmic motion. Their locked hypnotic eyes cause wonder as to which of the two leads the back-and-forth dance.

Wide-eyed spectators gasp when the cobra hisses and strikes. The man dodges the deadly fangs without skipping a note of his serenade. Again and again the snake strikes with lightning-quick movements, but the man pulls back out of reach. The tune grows softer and slower. Both stop swaying, and the snake sinks into its basket. After replacing the lid, the man smiles at the applauding audience. Coins are tossed onto his rug. The snake charmer's performance is over.

How do snake charmers do these unusual things? Music from a flute has nothing to do with the snake's actions during the show. A snake has no outer ears. It hears only a limited range of sounds carried by special bones in the snake's head. Not a music fan, the cobra simply responds to the movements of the flute player.

Sometimes a snake charmer is accused of removing the cobra's fangs. In other cases, the snake's mouth has been sewn shut! Even if the cobra does have visible fangs, perhaps the snake was "milked" of its venom before the performance. This is done by holding the snake's head and hooking the fangs over the edge of a glass vessel. Massaging the venom gland causes the poison to flow into the container.

No tricks are needed by some snake charmers. The man in the marketplace may rely on the snake's poor vision to make it miss its target. Or the snake charmer might know the cobra so well that he can judge its striking distance.

A professional snake charmer, also called a *fakir*, is sometimes trained at an academy near Delhi, India. Most of the students are members of the Hindu religion and consider the cobra to be a sacred animal.

They learn skills ranging from how to catch snakes to how to understand and handle them. Since cobras used for entertainment are not thrilled with the handling, they usually refuse to eat. A responsible fakir releases a cobra after a few weeks to prevent the snake from starving.

In North Africa, another type of snake charmer wows crowds. This performer is called a *haui*. The haui wraps an Egyptian cobra around his neck. He might even place the reptile's head in his mouth. Then he presses a spot someplace behind the snake's head, causing the cobra to become rigid. The motionless serpent seems to be in a hypnotic trance. Next the haui gently tosses the stiff snake to the ground and the cobra begins moving again. Baffled onlookers cheer.

In the mountains of Burma, a priestess of a snake cult "charms" a snake in a different way. The young girl performs a dance with one of the world's largest venomous snakes—the king cobra. This whopper grows up to 18 feet in length. Some king cobras can rise straight up to a height of over 4 feet, giving them an enormous striking range. Armed with fangs almost an inch long, a huge king cobra stores enough venom to kill an elephant. The ceremony begins when the king cobra emerges from a large container. After uttering special prayers, the young priestess approaches, bows to the big snake, and then begins to dance. The wary cobra rises nearly eye-to-eye with the girl.

This snake is not an ideal dance partner. Spreading its hood as a warning of danger, the snake flicks its forked tongue in and out. It strikes. The priestess steps quickly to one side and the cobra misses. Several times the aggressive snake attacks, but the girl dodges just in time. The confused serpent grows tired. The girl knows exactly when to elude the cobra's strike.

Suddenly, the priestess leans forward and kisses the cobra on its head. She draws away swiftly to avoid the strike that follows. Twice she repeats the death-tempting kiss before moving away from the angry snake. Afterwards, the king cobra is released into the nearby jungle. Incredibly, bites are rare during these dangerous religious ceremonies.

Asian and African countries are not alone in remarkable snake handling. A different type of event takes place each August in the United States. Snakes are important to the Hopi, a Native American tribe in the Southwest desert region. The snakes represent messengers between humans and the spirits. The Hopi ask the serpents to use special powers to bring rain and a good harvest.

After secret rituals, drumbeats begin. Hopi dancers shuffle around in a circle while chanting with a low humming sound. Pausing, they reach into a pit and grab snakes. Drumbeats quicken when the dancers continue with some snakes dangling from their mouths.

Among the snakes are full-grown rattlesnakes. Angry rattles threaten in a noisy choir of furious buzzing. Some of the snakes bite the dancers, but no one seems affected by the poison. One dancer presents a weird sight. A stretched-out rattler hangs by its fangs from the side of the man's face. The dancer is unfazed.

The Hopi protect their secrets, but it could be that the poisonous snakes have been "milked" before the rituals begin. Later, the snakes are set free in the desert.

Snakes are also used in religious ceremonies in remote areas of a few southern states. A Bible verse says, "they shall take up serpents." Some people take this very literally.

In the early 1900s, George Hensley, from Tennessee, founded a religion based on a strict conduct code. Hensley's followers believe they prove their faith by handling poisonous snakes. During church services, congregation members put themselves into delirious trances. They pick up writhing serpents from a box holding dozens of nasty-tempered copperheads and rattlesnakes.

Members have died from snakebites, but it's not a common occurrence. Hensley, the religion's founder, was bitten hundreds of times before a bite on his wrist by a diamondback rattler killed him in 1955. Some states now outlaw the religious custom of poisonous snake handling. Only a small number of isolated congregations still follow this dangerous practice.

Whether used for religious purposes or for entertainment, snake handling excites our curiosity. The interaction between people and venomous snakes is risky and unpredictable.

Snakes are creatures we do not ignore. Their unwavering stares intimidate us. And, their quick movements startle us when they slither, hiss, coil, or strike. Snakes terrify some of us, while others consider them fascinating. Either way, their bold defiance demands our respect.

We marvel at the daring of snake charmers. Their activities are far from dull or ordinary. Snake charmers safeguard their mystique by not sharing all of their secrets with us.

12

Why Can't We See Black Holes in Space?

How can we see the invisible? We can't see the wind, but we know it exists. We observe what the wind *does*. If we look through a telescope at the night sky, we can't see a black hole. But, scientists know they exist. They know this because of what a black hole *does*. It affects its surroundings.

No other objects in the universe are as mind-boggling as black holes. They spark new ideas about the very structure of the universe. Some people believe they will provide pathways to future space travel. Others claim that black holes might even lead to different universes! Science fiction fantasies? Maybe not. What is a black hole, anyway? First we must understand some basic things about gravity, mass, volume, and weight.

- **Gravity** is the force of attraction between two objects.
- **Mass** is the amount of matter in a body.
- **Volume** is the amount of space something occupies.

- **Weight** is a measure of the force of gravity pulling on a mass.

Over 300 years ago an English scientist named Isaac Newton watched an apple fall from a tree. Inspired by this simple observation, Newton used mathematics to describe gravity.

Scientists could now explain the force that keeps the moon orbiting the Earth. And they could begin to understand that the same forces determine the motions of planets and stars.

The farther apart two objects are, the weaker the gravity. As two objects grow closer, the gravity becomes stronger. The more massive object has stronger gravitational pull.

Two things might have the same volume, but differ greatly in mass. Stuff a pillowcase with fluffy popcorn; then stuff an identical pillowcase with sand. Particles of sand are crammed together more tightly than the matter of the popcorn. The sand is dense. More mass occupies the same amount of volume. The Earth's gravitational field pulls harder on the larger sand mass, so it weighs lots more than the popcorn.

If you step on a scale to be weighed, the scale is actually showing how hard the gravity of the Earth pulls on you. Astronauts in space become weightless. They are far enough from the Earth to escape the gravity. To leave the Earth's gravity, a rocket must speed more than 25,000 miles per hour to reach what is called an escape velocity.

In the early 1900s a genius named Albert Einstein shook the scientific world with his general theory of relativity. From Einstein's insights into the workings of our universe, astronomers and physicists drew dramatic conclusions. Among these was the theory that any object can become a black hole if it is dense enough.

Think of our Earth which has a diameter of almost 8,000 miles. Suppose you could shrink the entire planet to a diameter of just one inch. To make this miniature Earth, imagine how tightly mashed together the matter would be. All of the material in and on the Earth crunches together to occupy the space of a large marble. The heavy mass of the Earth is now squeezed so tightly that something strange happens. It becomes a black hole.

A black hole forms when an object's mass is packed together in such a small amount of volume that nothing escapes the force of its gravity. Although traveling 186,000 miles per second, not even light escapes.

The most probable theory of how a black hole is born involves the death of a gigantic star. Picture the explosion of a huge star that contains more than three times the mass of the Sun. The star erupts into a brilliant supernova giving off an incredible amount of energy. Eventually the center of the star shrinks.

When it reduces to a diameter of 60 miles or less, it becomes a neutron star. Gravity causes the matter to compress into a compacted dense mass. A single teaspoon of the dense matter would weigh a scale-busting 100 million tons on Earth! The neutron star continues collapsing until it becomes a "stellar" black hole.

Many astronomers think another type of black hole is at the center of most galaxies. These "supermassive" black holes swallow nearby stars. Our own Milky Way galaxy may contain this kind of black hole.

A third type of black hole is the "mini." A famous English physicist named Stephen Hawking offers new ways of thinking about mini black holes. They can have the heavy mass of a mountain jammed into the size of an atom. Hawking's ideas combine Einstein's general relativity with quantum theory, the physics of very tiny particles.

Even large black holes cannot be seen, but scientists describe what they might be like. Think of a black hole as a cosmic whirlpool. It swirls like water draining out of a sink, picking up nearby objects and funneling them into its center.

Near the surface edge of the activity is the *event horizon*. This is where light can no longer escape. All matter coming into contact with the event horizon is at the mercy of the black hole's gravity. Scientists think

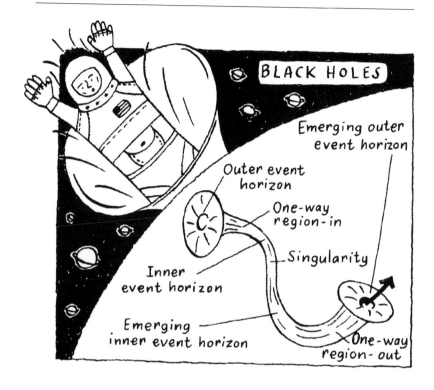

that inside the black hole matter is ripped apart, surrendering its energy to the black hole's feeding frenzy.

In the center of the black hole is the *singularity*. At this stage everything disappears from our universe. Gravity is so strong that the mass is crushed into a point with no diameter at all. How can something become nothing? Where does the matter go? No one knows. Scientists study, ponder, talk, debate . . . but no one knows for certain what happens to the matter that is pulled into the singularity of a black hole.

Science fiction writers love this kind of thing. No

concrete answers, so anything goes. Scientists themselves propose sensational ideas about the singularity. This is where the notion of *wormholes* comes in.

Let's take a wild ride with our imaginations. Outfitted in a space suit, you are drifting along somewhere out in space. You approach a black hole. Moving faster and faster, you reach the speed of light at the event horizon. The intense gravity begins to pull you out of shape. Falling feet first into the black hole, your body stretches out like a piece of spaghetti. Scientists actually refer to this as "spaghettification."

If you've entered a huge rotating black hole, maybe you can survive the singularity. You sweep through it like passing through a doughnut hole. Perhaps this black hole is hooked up to a second, mirror-image, black hole. You tunnel through then exit the other end (a white hole) into another universe. You've just traveled through a wormhole.

In the mid-1980s an American physicist named Kip Thorne suggested that wormholes could be used like this for future space travel.

Nonsense, say critics. All the particles of matter that make you up would be ripped apart when the powerful gravity first pulls you across the event horizon. It seems likely that would happen, but no one knows for sure. Exactly what goes on inside the black hole is a mystery. Scientists offer guesses, but no proof.

Until recently, some scientists were not even convinced that black holes existed. But others did believe in them. Believers pointed to likely candidates—black holes surrounded by swirling gases giving off X-rays (tiny high energy particles). When matter from a nearby star falls into a black hole, X-rays are given off by the hot gases before they disappear forever. Satellites detect these X-rays.

Then in 1994 the Hubble Space Telescope helped astronomers confirm the existence of a black hole. They found it in the core of the huge galaxy called M87, which is fifty million light years away. (One light year is nearly six trillion miles.) In the heart of this enormous galaxy lies a colossal black hole with the mass of three billion Suns. Astronomers were alerted by a disk of hot gases, spinning violently, held together by what could only be a black hole's gravity. Since then, the telescope has helped identify many other black holes.

The Hubble Space Telescope also provides a glimpse into regions at the edge of our known universe. We peek at galaxies considered to be ten billion light years away. The Hubble Space Telescope is one of the many tools that will pry open secrets of our enormous universe.

We baby-step toward an understanding of black holes. Secrets held inside them are beyond our current knowledge of physics. Some scientists say that solving the riddle of black holes is the key to understanding the universe itself.

All of us dream about the future. We hear the prediction that wormholes will give us shortcuts to distant points in space. A far-fetched idea? What seems like "strange stuff" to us today may become commonplace to our great-great-great-grandchildren.

What a wondrous time this is! Exciting discoveries wait to be revealed. Threads of ideas that puzzle us now will someday weave amazingly clear patterns.

Each day our knowledge expands. But if we need a reminder of how little we still know, we can gaze at the dark sky on a clear moonless night. Billions of glittering stars beckon us to explore the unknown, beyond our speck of a planet.

Bibliography

Chapter 1. How Dangerous Is Quicksand?

Bauman, Richard. "Quicksand: Nature's Sinister Booby Trap." *Cricket Magazine* (August 1995): 22–23.

dePaola, Tomie. *The Quicksand Book*. New York: Holiday House, 1977.

Parker, Ronald B. *Inscrutable Earth*. New York: Charles Scribner's Sons, 1984.

Ware, Leslie. "Quicksand: Makes a Good Story." *Audubon Magazine* 92, no. 3 (May 1990): 126–132.

Willis, Willma. *Sand and Man*. Chicago: Childrens Press, 1973.

Chapter 2. Is Bigfoot a Big Joke?

Ancient Mysteries Documentary: "Bigfoot." Arts and Entertainment Television Channel. Video, 1994.

Aylesworth, Thomas G. *Science Looks at Mysterious Monsters*. New York: Julian Messner, 1982.

Christian, Mary Blount. *The Mystery of Bigfoot*. Mankato, Minn.: Crestwood House, 1987.

Cohen, Daniel. *Monster Hunting Today*. New York: Dodd, Mead & Co., 1983.

Gaffron, Norma. *Bigfoot: Opposing Viewpoints*. San Diego, Calif.: Greenhaven Press, 1989.

Odor, Ruth Shannon. *Bigfoot*. Chicago: Childrens Press, 1989.

Wyatt, J. Michael. "The Bigfoot Primer." *Backpacker Magazine* 18, no. 5 (August 1990): 62–65.

Chapter 3. Does the Bermuda Triangle Deserve Its Bad Reputation?

Abels, Harriett Sheffer. *Bermuda Triangle*. Mankato, Minn: Crestwood House, 1987.

Bibliography

Berlitz, Charles. *The Bermuda Triangle*. New York: Doubleday & Co., Inc., 1974.

Dolan, Edward F. *The Bermuda Triangle and Other Mysteries of Nature*. New York: Franklin Watts, 1980.

Floyd, E. Randall. *Great American Mysteries*. Little Rock, Ark.: August House Publishers, Inc., 1991.

Gaffron, Norma. *The Bermuda Triangle: Opposing Viewpoints*. San Diego, Calif.: Greenhaven Press, 1995.

HarperCollins Publishers, Ltd. *Unsolved Mysteries*. Mankato, Minn.: Creative Education, 1997.

Kusche, Lawrence. *The Disappearance of Flight 19*. New York: Harper & Row, 1980.

Sheaffer, Robert. "Methane Missiles & Comet Tales." *Skeptical Inquirer Magazine* 21, no. 2 (March/April 1997): 23–24.

Chapter 4. What Do You Feed a Carnivorous (Meat-Eating) Plant?

Aaseng, Nathan. *Meat-Eating Plants*. Springfield, N.J.: Enslow Publishers, Inc., 1996.

Cooper, Jason. *Insect-Eating Plants*. Vero Beach, Fla.: Rourke Enterprises, Inc., 1991.

Editors, *The Economist*. "A Tiny Tender Trap: Carnivorous Plants." *The Economist* 346, no. 8062 (April 4, 1998): 86–87.

Lerner, Carol. *Pitcher Plants: The Elegant Insect Traps*. New York: William Morrow and Company, 1983.

Overbeck, Cynthia. *Carnivorous Plants*. Minneapolis: Lerner Publications Company, 1982.

Wexler, Jerome. *Sundew Stranglers: Plants That Eat Insects*. New York: Dutton Children's Books, 1995.

Chapter 5. What Are Feral Children?

Botkin, B.A., ed. *The Treasury of American Folklore*. New York: Crown Publishers, 1944.

Burger, John R., and Lewis Gardner. *Children of the Wild.* New York: Julian Messner, 1979.

Candland, Douglas Keith. *Feral Children and Clever Animals.* New York: Oxford University Press, 1993.

Itard, Jean-Marc-Gaspard. *The Wild Boy of Aveyron.* New York: Appleton-Century-Crofts, 1962.

Landau, Elaine. *Wild Children: Growing Up Without Human Contact.* Danbury, Conn.: Franklin Watts, Inc., 1998.

Lane, Harlan, and Richard Pillard. *The Wild Boy of Burundi.* New York: Random House, 1978.

Shattuck, Roger. *The Forbidden Experiment: The Story of the Wild Boy of Aveyron.* New York: Farrar Straus Giroux, 1980.

Walsh, Jill Paton. *Knowledge of Angels.* New York: Houghton Mifflin Company, 1994.

Wootton, Anthony. *Animal Folklore, Myth and Legend.* New York: Blandford Press, 1986.

Chapter 6. Why Do Treasure Hunters Keep Digging Up Oak Island?

Barber, Nicola. *The Search for Gold.* Austin, Tex.: Raintree Steck-Vaughn Publishers, 1998.

O'Connor, D'Arcy. *The Money Pit.* New York: Coward, McCann & Geoghegan, Inc., 1978.

Preston, Douglas. "Death Trap Defies Treasure Seekers for Two Centuries." *Smithsonian Magazine* 19, no. 3 (June 1988): 52–63.

Proctor, Steve. "Island of Controversy." *Maclean's Magazine* 108, no. 34 (August 21, 1995): 54.

Schwartz, Alvin. *Gold & Silver, Silver & Gold.* New York: Farrar Straus Giroux, 1989.

Taylor, Michael. "Yep, They're Still Digging." A supplement to *Forbes Magazine* (September 25, 1995): 138–142.

Bibliography

Chapter 7. Who's Afraid of Voodoo and Zombies?

Beckwith, Carol, and Angela Fisher. "The African Roots of Voodoo." *National Geographic Magazine* 166, no. 2 (August 1995): 102–113.

Cohen, Daniel. *Raising the Dead.* New York: Cobblehill Books, 1997.

Davis, Wade. *The Serpent and the Rainbow.* New York: Simon and Schuster, 1985.

Haskins, James. *Witchcraft, Mysticism and Magic in the Black World.* New York: Doubleday & Co., Inc., 1974.

Kristos, Kyle. *Voodoo.* New York: J.B. Lippincott Company, 1976.

Kurlansky, Mark. "Voodoo Heart." *Travel Holiday Magazine* 179, no. 9 (November 1996): 70–74.

Littlewood, Roland, and Chavannes Douyon. "Clinical Findings in Three Cases of Zombification." *The Lancet Magazine* 350, no. 9084 (October 11, 1997): 1094–1096.

Chapter 8. Do Mermaids Exist?

Bright, Michael. *There Are Giants in the Sea.* London, England: Robson Books, 1989.

Climo, Shirley. *A Treasury of Mermaids: Mermaid Tales from Around the World.* New York: HarperCollins Publishers, 1997.

Editors, Reader's Digest. *Quest for the Unknown: Man and Beast.* New York: The Reader's Digest Association, Inc., 1993.

Ellis, Richard. *Monsters of the Sea.* New York: Doubleday, 1995.

Kovacs, Deborah and Kate Madin. *Beneath Blue Waters: Meetings with Remarkable Deep-Sea Creatures.* New York: Viking, 1996.

Nicholson, Robert. *Great Mysteries.* New York: Thompson Learning, 1995.

Chapter 9. What's Creepier—a Scorpion or a Tarantula?

Cooper, Jason. *Scorpions: Animals Without Bones.* Vero Beach, Fla.: Rourke Publications, Inc., 1996.

Gerholdt, James E. *Tarantula Spiders.* Edina, Minn.: Abdo & Daughters, 1996.

Martin, Louise. *Tarantulas*. Vero Beach, Fla.: Rourke Enterprises, Inc., 1988.

McAuliffe, Emily. *Tarantulas*. New York: RiverFront Books, 1998.

Murray, Peter. *Scorpions*. Chicago: The Child's World, Inc., 1997.

Murray, Peter. *Tarantulas*. Chicago: The Child's World, Inc., 1993.

Pringle, Lawrence. *Scorpion Man: Exploring the World of Scorpions*. New York: Charles Scribner's Sons, 1994.

Tesar, Jenny. *Spiders*. Woodbridge, Conn.: Blackbirch Press, Inc., 1993.

Chapter 10. What Happened to Atlantis?

Abels, Harriette. *The Lost City of Atlantis*. New York: Crestwood House, 1987.

Berlitz, Charles. *Atlantis, The Eighth Continent*. New York: G.P. Putnam's Sons, 1984.

Braymer, Marjorie. *Atlantis*. New York: Atheneum (A Margaret K. McElderry Book), 1983.

Cottrell, Leonard. *Lost Civilizations*. New York: Franklin Watts, Inc., 1974.

David, Lester. "Atlantis Destroyed." *Boys' Life Magazine* (September 1995): 26–29.

Gallant, Roy A. *Lost Cities*. New York: Franklin Watts, 1985.

Joseph, Francis. *The Destruction of Atlantis*. Chicago: Atlantis Research Publishers, 1987.

Muck, Otto. *The Secret of Atlantis*. New York: Times Books, 1976.

Simon, Seymour. *Strange Mysteries From Around the World*. New York: Morrow Junior Books, 1997.

Tompkins, Ptolemy. "Lost Atlantis." *Harper's Magazine* (January 1997): 76–83.

Wilson, Colin. *From Atlantis to the Sphinx*, New York: Fromm International Publishing Co., 1996.

Bibliography

Chapter 11. Do Snake Charmers Really Charm Snakes?

Beit-Hallahmi, Benjamin. *The Illustrated Encyclopedia of Active New Religions, Sects, and Cults.* New York: The Rosen Publishing Group, Inc., 1998.

Dewey, Jennifer Owens. *Rattlesnake Dance: True Tales, Mysteries, and Rattlesnake Ceremonies.* Honesdale, Pa.: Boyds Mills Press, Inc., 1997.

Editors, Reader's Digest. *Man and Beast: Quest for the Unknown.* New York: The Reader's Digest Association, Inc., 1993.

Engelmann, Wolf-Eberhard, and Fritz Jurgen Obst. *Snakes: Biology, Behavior and Relationship to Man.* New York: Exeter Books, 1981.

Green, Carl R., and William R. Sanford. *The Cobra.* Mankato, Minn.: Crestwood House, 1986.

McDonald, Mary Ann. *Rattlesnakes.* Minneapolis: Capstone Press, 1996.

Nissenson, Marilyn, and Susan Jonas. *Snake Charm.* New York: Harry N. Abrams, Inc., 1995.

Chapter 12. Why Can't We See Black Holes in Space?

Asimov, Isaac. *Mysteries of Deep Space: Black Holes, Pulsars, and Quasars.* Milwaukee, Wisc.: Gareth Stevens Publishing, 1994.

Begelman, Mitchell C., and Martin Rees. *Gravity's Fatal Attraction: Black Holes in the Universe.* New York: Scientific American Library, 1996.

Couper, Heather, and Nigel Henbest. *Black Holes.* New York: Dorling Kindersly Publishing, 1996.

Newton, David E. *Secrets of Space: Black Holes and Supernovae.* New York: Twenty-First Century Books, 1997.

Petersen, Carolyn Collins, and John C. Brandt. *Hubble Vision: Astronomy with the Hubble Space Telescope.* Cambridge, England: Cambridge University Press, 1995.

Trefil, James. "Black Holes: Hubble Sheds Light." *USA Weekend Magazine* (May 15–17, 1998): 11.

Index

Index